CONFLUENCES
The Narratives Show

S. David

Copyright ©2008 by S. David

All rights reserved. No part of this publication may be reproduced,
stored in a retrieval system or transmitted in any form or
by any means electronic, mechanical, photocopying, recording
or otherwise, without the prior written permission of the publisher.

Published by The Skaldic Soul
in cooperation with The Brooklyn Waterfront Artists Coalition
Brooklyn, New York

Design and layout: Julie Unruh
Front cover photograph: Gary Heller, *Pot of Gold in Red Hook, Brooklyn* (detail)
Back cover photograph: Brandon Emerick, video still from *Poetry and Paintings*:
http://blip.tv/file/764797

International Standard Book Number (ISBN)
paper: 978-0-615-25515-6

Printed in the United States of America

Table of contents

4	Foreword
5	Introduction
6	Open Book
8	The Vanquished
10	Fence
12	Traces
14	Waiting for the Bus
16	Deity in Manhattan
18	Reddyteddy Bear
20	Stickball
22	The Boys
24	One Man's Fantasy
26	Hourglass Figure
28	Are You Going to Heaven?
30	Deep Thoughts
32	2 Anonymous Women
34	Behold
36	Boudoir & Dreams
38	Gigs Thurs, Fri, Sat.
40	Stubborn
42	Nocturne
44	Foolishly
46	Cut-Off
48	Reflections
50	Your Name is Spring
52	American Gothic Mice
54	Play
56	Balance Act
58	Woman with Stick
60	Woman with Frogs
62	The King
64	Vanitas
66	Frustration
68	The Eye
70	The Sage
72	The Light
74	Turtle Under the Sky
76	Slay the Myth
78	Serene Demons
81	Acknowledgements
83	Artists

Foreword

S. David loves to look at art and find his truths in it.

This slim volume unites two forms of art and so is a treasure because it is the first of its kind, as far as I know. For it unites the visual world of art with the spiritual symbolic world of poetry and words.

These poems were motivated, and came to life, by S. David's observation and reaction to art works which were on exhibition at BWAC (Brooklyn Waterfront Artists Coalition) art shows at the pier in Red Hook, Brooklyn.

As S. David looks at an art work, he does not judge it as to its perfection in technique, or virtuosity, but rather if it speaks to him: is there a deeper meaning, a tale that is obscure, that he can unravel and emphasize and so enrich the experience?

Perhaps by his words he can and will open new doors of perception for the viewers' enjoyment of the art works.

Anna Annus-Hagen
Vice President, BWAC

Introduction

It all depends on how we look at art. We can see it so many ways and I say we can even hear it, we can smell it, we can taste it, we can see it as we could see music, as colors. I'm reminded of Laura Nyro; she could see music as colors, she would see pitch, range, the orchestration, but she never wrote down notes, she could tell them, 'play it like a wooden chair. Play green. Play it bronze.' Which is, I think, a disease called synesthesia, but hell, we should look at art with more than one sense. As for my poetry, I don't know what comes out when I look at art until I've written it. I actually read it afterwards. I mean none of this is actually crafted; it's all what came out as I looked at the piece. So I walk around – some of you have seen my sack, I have pictures, I've taken them at shows, most of them – and then I'll pull them out, and I'll wait for some of them to speak. They'll say 'okay, here's where we're going,' and then [chi chi chi chi chi - writing noises]. I've been told it works, that's the 'why' of this book. I know of one other person in the world who works with many artists, she's in Portugal. There are poets who work with an artist; there are poets who are artists. There are artists who are poets, there are musicians who are poets, blah blah blah blah blah. But as far as working with many artists, there's the two of us. And I want to thank the so-many artists whose works have been my Muse: this is really about them.

S. David

Open Book

The pen lay capped
Quills had been
Replaced
A single moment
Of time
As the Scribe
Shook loose
A knot in His arm
Cracked His knuckles
The Book lay open
A fresh blank page
The moment passed
His Hand picked up
The pen
Scribed
New names
Onto the sheet
Yet for one
Single minute
No one anywhere
Died

Debra P. Hershkowitz
pen paper porcelain
Black and white photograph using high-speed negative film
8.5" x 5.5"

The Vanquished

Cold weather
Battle fought
Battle lost
Beaten
Retreating
Faces showing
The emotions
Despair
Bitterness
Anger
And fear
Look at them
Look into
Their eyes
These are
The vanquished
Study
What you see
Is surrender
An option

Richard Ekelund
The Vanquished
Conte crayon on paper
34" x 17"

Fence

Boundaries
Real
Physical
Mental
Behavior
Property
Even safety
And fences
Are built
To keep some
Out
And others
In
But some
Just don't
Give a damn
Crossing
Willfully
Often
Getting hurt

Robert Marvin
Fence, Grafton, Vermont
Silver Gelatin Print
14" x 11"

Traces

Inspiration drawn
From where
Wherever
Even the simplest things
Anywhere you can find
Traces of things
Different
A bottle of booze
A box of cigars
A sandwich
You don't care
You're an artist

Gerard Barbot
Traces
Collage
4" x 6"

Waiting for the Bus

Regimented
By chance
By choice
Working
Nine to fives
Like lemmings
Rushing to wait
For their buses
Mass suicide
Of the mind
Welcome to
A two fare
Urban
Neighborhood

Gerard Enright
Meercats Waiting for the Bus
Digital photograph
7.75" x 11"

Deity in Manhattan

Walking down
A Manhattan street
Oh some months ago
And it was filled with
Women young women
Rushing here rushing
There and school and
Careers and I'm thinking
How many of them have
No time in their lives
For relationships and
Yet Heaven forefend
But do not call me sexist
For there were some
Who looked like true
Earth mothers and I
Thought "you ought to be
Pregnant" I remembered
One face and here
I was again yesterday
And Ganesh must have
Overheard for I recognized
The woman coming
Down that same street
And she was

Arden Suydam
Deity in Manhattan
Photograph
8" x 10"

Reddyteddy Bear

Did you have one
One you took
Everywhere
When you were
A toddler
And a few years
Beyond
Did your mother
Throw it away
When a seam
Burst or did you
Put him on a shelf
Real
A friend you put
Away but one that
Was always ready
To play or let you
Dream
In his world
Did you have one
I did too

Alfred Ingegno
Reddy teddy
Oil on canvas board
24" x 30"

Stickball

Brooklyn or elsewhere
In N.Y. City
I don't know
      About
      Other
      Places
The time
The fifties
The sixties
The seventies
Did it continue
Into the eighties
And not sewer ball
Stickball and no catcher
Off one wall onto another
Across the street
Mop broom the handle
The stick and a Spaldeen
This mop died
For you
And your mother
Was not
Happy

Philip Van Cott
Stickball
Oil on hardwood
12" x 12"

The Boys

Growing up blue
Collar ethnic city
Boys from the hood
Knowing what is and
Isn't good and having
A good time with
The guys beers smokes
And broads and some
Tit and porn shows
Coming of age rites
Graduating high school
Was the big deal
Now you can call them
The vanishing Americans
But then hey has it
Really changed prices
Have but the rituals

George Stainback
Fun with the Boys
Collage, Photography
32" x 24"

One Man's Fantasy

Recognition
Fame but more
Than that what
He wanted was
Simply women
Screaming his name
All wanting a piece
Of him the right piece

Craig Howarth
One Man's Fantasy
Paper and acrylic collage on Yupo
6" x 6"

Hourglass Figure

Friday night
At eight
Ah what pleasure
Fall summer spring
Dressed to impress
Dressed for hunting
And they parade
In heels down
The street and
Men are watching
The hourglass
Figures on display

Jillian Kulka
Hourglass Figure
Mixed media
4.75" x 7"

Are You Going to Heaven?

I watched her
Walk down the street
Passing the Holy Roller's
Table by the curb and
Reading their sign
I got religion
"Oh my God woman"
I thought "Woman
Come be with me
The answer is easy
You with me yes
Yes I am that easy
And I've found
Heaven on earth
And if I then die yes
Yes either way
You mine and I'm
Going to Heaven"
She passed me by
I never said a word

Liz Johnson
Are You Going To Heaven?
Acrylic on canvas
2.5" x 5" (oval)

Deep Thoughts

I can't speak
For the female
Mind but the deep
Thoughts on his
Were obvious
Too obvious
He
Was
Betrayed
By the leer
On his face

Craig Howarth
Deep Thoughts
Paper and acrylic collage on Yupo
6" x 6"

Two Anonymous Women

Alright
Where are they
Why are you
Flaunting
Their picture
In my face
Why make them
Why are they
Anonymous
Would I
Recognize them
Or are they
Truly
Where then
Are they hiding
Where did you
Find them
Can I

Carlo Grassini
Two Anonymous Women
Oil stick on 100% cotton paper
22" x 30"

Behold

She loved
The adrenal rush
Playing with
Danger
Was what
Her life was
About
And his eyes
Those eyes

Anujan Ezhikode
Behold
Acrylic on canvas
12" x 12"

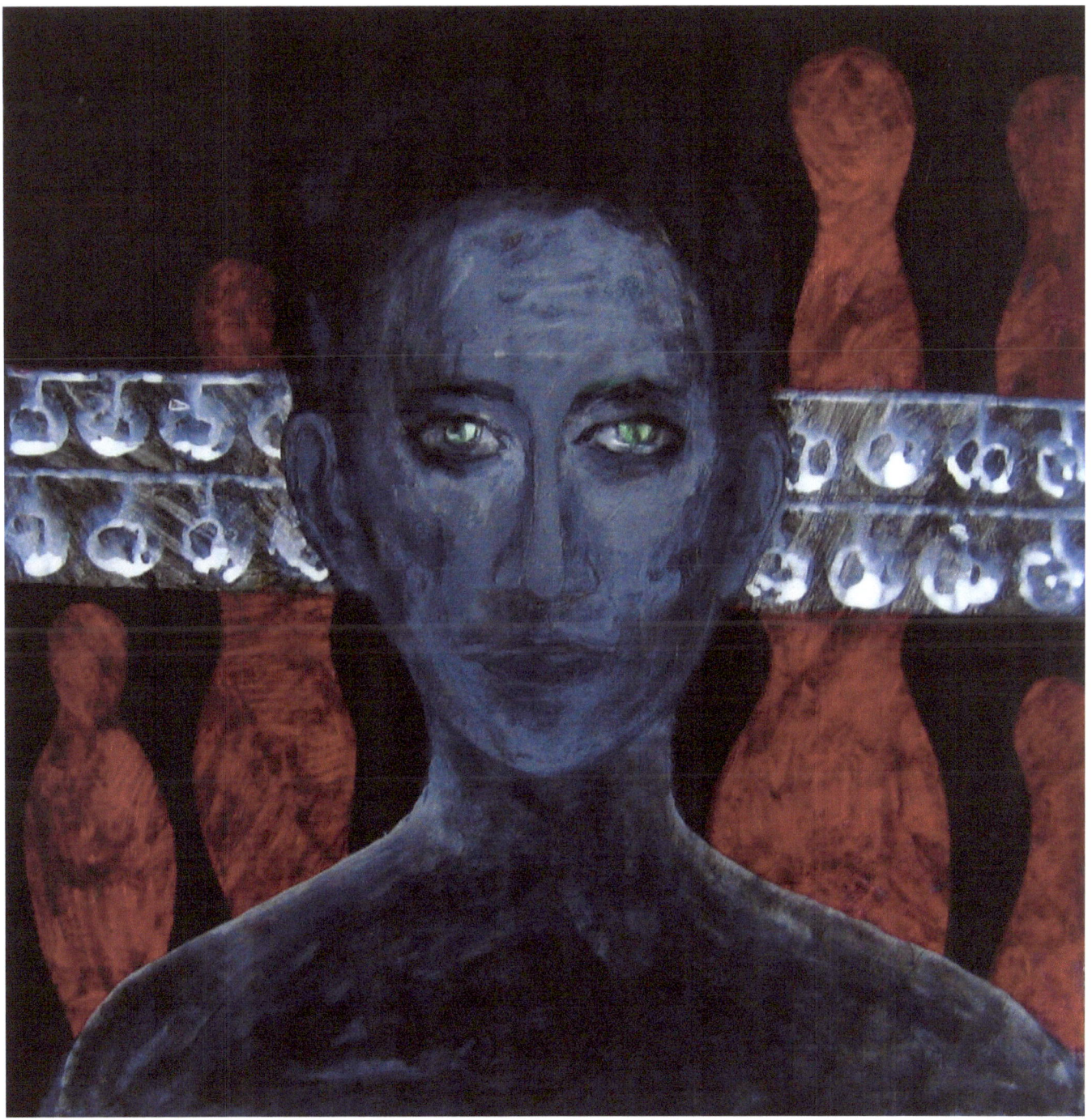

Boudoir & Dreams

The bed was ready
Though she awaited him
Downstairs on a couch
And he was late
She fell asleep waiting
When he arrived
He tiptoed past her
In the morning
She found him
Sleeping in the bed
That's when she...

Priscilla Bain-Smith
Boudoir and Dreams
Paper collage (non-digital)
8" x 10"
Collection of Ellie Winberg

Gigs Thurs, Fri, Sat.

Can't take her out
Anymore she's working
Social night gigs
Thursday Friday
Saturday nights
Not being selfish
The other nights
She's rehearsing
Two bands and
Practice it was fun
But new demands
On her time meant
No time for us
I was working days

Liz Longo
Gigs Thurs, Fri, Sat.
Oil on canvas
15" x 30"

Stubborn

It's true
It may have been
Even love but
Anyway "I liked her
Very much"
Unusual bright
Quite lovely but
"She was rigid and
Stubborn" yet our time
Together was interesting
When we met I was
Ambivalent for a while
But "whatever she wanted
To do she was going
To do" and I was what
She was going to do
For a while and
On and off she had power
The power of 'yes'
But I was stubborn too
And I had the power of 'no'

Suzanne Sheridan
Stubborn
Mixed media on paper
22" x 30"

Nocturne

Play me
A long and
Sad song
This night
You've done
Your best
To ruin
My rest
So many
Nights just
Pass by you
Pulling away
Going away
Were you
Ever here
With me

Yuri Y. Yurov
Nocturne
Photograph
16"x24"

Foolishly

Wise
Knowing men
Their ways
Well
That's what her friends
Felt came to her
For advice
Consolation
And she was
Until
Sitting with him
She knew
She could hurt
Or be hurt
She turned
To him
Told him
"You're good
And I well
Foolishly I
Took the bait
Pull me in
Or let me go"
He let her go
She did not
Mourn the parting

Suzanne Sheridan
Foolishly
Mixed media on paper
30" x 22"

Cut-Off

It's American Urban
Not American Gothic
True to life
But just as
The computer
Began its mad reign
And it isn't strange
That their relationship
Became a total mess
She cut him off
And as a smack
In the face posted
The cut-off and
Her availability
On Match.com

Russell Mehlman
Cut-off
Oil on canvas
11" x 14"

Reflections

That's where he went
Into memories and
Reflecting on images
Reflections of his past
The present sucked
He was really
Falling apart
And safety lay
In reflections
The day to day
Had become
Impossible
To handle
Why
That's his story
To tell not mine

Nancy Rodrigo
Reflections
Mixed media on canvas with photograph
12" x 16"

Your Name Is Spring

Winter was due next
The season my time
Short days
Long nights
Cold nights
Slower and
Slowing still
And dreaming
Daydreaming
Missing summer
Losing fall
Hoping
But hoping
Leaves people
Powerless
Needing
To move
To try
So go
Trying
Happening
Chance
Fate
So I turned to her
Your name is Spring

Annette Jaret
Your Name Is Spring
Watercolor and ink on paper
24" x 18"

American Gothic Mice

Still in a world
Of 'what if'
A world of
Parody
There is dignity
It was across
A dimension rift
In a replica
Of this world
Dominated
By the rodent ilk
As the simian branch
Never developed
A farmer and
His daughter
Posed for their picture

Alan F. Beck
American Gothic Mice
Watercolor
4" x 6"
Private Collection

Play

Copulation between
Angels leads to cherubim
And play's just the thing
To keep them from bedeviling
The parental generation or
Interfering with their duties
And playrooms in the Heavenly
Mansion provide many
Distractions yet a full bathtub
Is an extra fun outlet for
Cherubic exuberance

Stephen Basso
Play
Oil on board
20"x 26"

Balance Act

Not fair
Not fair at all
A show off
Goofing on
Us common folk
A balance act
Is not hard
To do when
You've got wings

Anujan Ezhikode
Balance Act
Acrylic on canvas
34 " x 48"

Woman with Stick

Go back
Way back
Before then
Before cities
Back when
And then when
A good piece
Of wood was
A walking stick
A carrier pole
A tool
A weapon
And she was
Armed and
Dangerous

Laurent Jacquinot
Untitled
Pencil on vellum
7.5" x 11"

Woman with Frogs

Upset
It didn't work
Not the way
It was supposed
To work
Too many frogs
Kissed
None turned
Into princes
One prince
She kissed
Naturally
Turned into
A frog

Imelda Fagin
Woman with Frogs
Acrylic on canvas
6" x 12"

The King

Regal bearing
Proud
Every inch
A King
Every inch
A fit ruler
For his people
For his kind
There he stands
Waiting
For his people
For his subjects
To stand
Before him
Acknowledging
Him kneeling
Ah royalty

Larry Scaturro
The King
Walnut
34" x 7" x 7"

Vanitas

Does it matter
Or are you one
Who needs your body
Together at the End
Of Days and those
Who have turned
To dust what of them
Their souls have
Traveled the Path
Set out for them

So what if your
Skull ends as
A paperweight
In some collector's
Den he too will
One day join you

Luis Soler
Vanitas
Oil on canvas
24" x 20"
Private collection

Frustration

Seeing too much
Too too much and
You know because
You understand
You wish it was
Going to be different
But you see Too Much
And frustration grows
Tired weary and all around
You blurs for you see
Tomorrows beyond today
And it is still the same

Gabriela Vasa
Frustration
Acrylic and modeling paste
on canvas
30" x 24"

The Eye

Take this eye
From the top
Of the pyramid
Still it sees all
There are no
Tears here
Rather
A Seeing
The world
As it is
As it will be
A Seer's eye
Without
A voice

Darrin Da Grossa
The Eye
Oil on canvas
24" x 18"

The Sage

He knows
He does not know
But he seeks
Seeking
Understanding
This is his Truth
He has sought
To understand
All his life
Thus he is marked
Thus he is known
And many come
Seeking him
To learn
What he understands

Dorothy Schaffner
The Sage
Watercolor and gold leaf on paper
6" x 9"

The Light

But it's so dark
And his light
Is so small
Barely a glow
In that darkness
Of the night
Surrounding him
Yet it is light
Perhaps enough
To keep him from
Stumbling as he
Makes his way
Perhaps

Faith Gabel
The Light
Acrylic on canvas
18" x 24"

The Turtle Under the Sky

But he carries
A world
The world
On his back
No not Atlas
He is the Creator's
Creation
So it is told
So it is given
Amongst the People
From the primal
Sea he emerged
Mystery upon
Mystery
The Chinese
Tell the story
Of the river
Turtle emerging
With a magic square
Upon his back
Tribal people here
Tell the greater tale
But all is Maya

Yuri Y. Yurov
The Turtle Under the Skies
Acrylic paste, oil on canvas
40" x 32"

Slay the Myth

Slay the myth
Kill the fantasy
Destroy the illusion
Legends are dangerous
So the storyteller died
Now he comes
It is time
Let us stone
The poet

Gerard Barbot
Slay the Myth
Collage
4" x 6"

Serene Demons

Well done
I say
Well done
And now
Take your rest
In the warmth
And the glow
Of the fires
Of Hell
You've given
The world above
A solid blow
And each of you
Contributed well

So they were told
So these demons
Rested so serene
In the bowels
Of Hell

Darcy Merante
Serene Demons
Enamel on steel mounted on wood
8" x 8"

Acknowledgements

I really didn't want to do this book. These poems represent my personal experiences with these artists' works. I've shared them with the artists involved and thought, "well that's that." But I've constantly been asked to also share my poetry with others. BWAC invited me in 2006 to become part of a program called "Artist Speaks" and as of this writing, I've read poetry under and separately from that program at seven shows. I was asked to do a similar reading to close the 9th annual Williamsburg Art Salon of the Williamsburg Art and Historical Center. That reading was videotaped by both the Center and Brandon Emerick (sdavid.blip.tv). A BWAC artist, Julie Unruh, demanded that I do a book and said she would do most of the non-poetry work involved, so what you hold in your hand is actually a collaboration. You'll notice there's no work by Julie here, so this has been quite selfless on her part and my truest thanks go to her.

S. David

Notes

Artists

S. David	theskaldicsoul.com
Priscilla Bain-Smith	priscilla.bain-smith.brooklynartist.com
Gerard Barbot	gerard.barbot.brooklynartist.com
Stephen Basso	bassostephen@gmail.com
Alan F. Beck	alanfbeck.com
Darrin Da Grossa	dpdart.com
Richard Ekelund	rekelund@si.rr.com
Gerard Enright	ennybabe1329@aol.com
Anujan Ezhikode	anujanezhikode.com
Imelda Fagin	imeldafagin.com
Faith Gabel	faith.gabel.brooklynartist.com
Carlo Grassini	grassini.artlog.com
Debra P. Hershkowitz	debra.hershkowitz.brooklynartist.com
Craig Howarth	craighowarth.com
Alfred Ingegno	alfred.ingegno.brooklynartist.com
Laurent Jacquinot	ljacquinot@yahoo.co.uk
Annette Jaret	annette.jaret.brooklynartist.com
Liz Johnson	liz.johnson.brooklynartist.com
Jillian Kulka	artistjillk@yahoo.com
Liz Longo	liz.longo.brooklynartist.com
Robert Marvin	fgpo.org/gallery/
Russell Mehlman	russellmehlman.com
Darcy Merante	darcymerante.com
Nancy Rodrigo	nancy.rodrigo.brooklynartist.com
Larry Scaturro	scaturrowoodworks.com
Dorothy Schaffner	
Suzanne Sheridan	myspace.com/9suzie
Luis Soler	luis_soler2002@yahoo.com
George Stainback	ncreativecompany.50megs.com
Arden Suydam	347-677-4816
Philip Van Cott	philipvancott.com
Gabriela Vasa	gabriela.vasa.brooklynartist.com
Yuri Y. Yurov	yyyurov.com

Covers:

Gary Heller	garyhellerphotography.com
Brandon Emerick	electromedia.blip.tv
Brooklyn Waterfront Artists Coalition	bwac.org

www.ingramcontent.com/pod-product-compliance
Lightning Source LLC
Chambersburg PA
CBHW041537220426
43663CB00002B/62